Whose Work Is This?

**A Look at Things
Animals Make—
Pearls, Milk, and Honey**

Written by Nancy Kelly Allen

Illustrated by Derrick Alderman
and Denise Shea

PICTURE WINDOW BOOKS
Minneapolis, Minnesota

Whose
Is It?
Science

Special thanks to our advisers for their expertise:

Debbie Folkerts, Ph.D.
Assistant Professor of Biological Sciences
Auburn University, Alabama

Susan Kesselring, M.A., Literacy Educator
Rosemount-Apple Valley-Eagan (Minnesota) School District

Managing Editors: Bob Temple, Catherine Neitge
Creative Director: Terri Foley
Editors: Nadia Higgins, Patricia Stockland
Editorial Adviser: Andrea Cascardi
Storyboard Development: Amy Bailey Muehlenhardt
Designer: Nathan Gassman
Page production: Banta
The illustrations in this book were prepared digitally.

Picture Window Books
5115 Excelsior Boulevard
Suite 232
Minneapolis, MN 55416
877-845-8392
www.picturewindowbooks.com

Printed in the United States of America.

Library of Congress Cataloging-in-Publication Data
Allen, Nancy Kelly, 1949-
Whose work is this? : a look at things animals make—pearls, milk,
and honey / by Nancy Kelly Allen ; illustrated by Derrick Alderman
and Denise Shea.
p. cm. — (Whose is it?)
Includes bibliographical references (p.   ).
ISBN 1-4048-0612-1 (reinforced library binding)
1. Animal behavior—Juvenile literature. I. Alderman, Derrick, ill.
II. Shea, Denise, ill. III. Title. IV. Series.

QL751.5.A44 2004
591.5—dc22   2004000883

Let's get to work, and see who's who.

Look closely at something an animal has made. Animals make things that help them live better. They make food to feed their babies. They make cozy homes. They make poison to kill their prey.

People turn animals' work into useful products. An animal's work can sweeten pies and cakes. It can be used to make beautiful jewelry. It can even make life-saving medicine.

Can you tell whose work is whose?

Look in the back for more fun facts about the work animals do.

Whose work is this,
dripping so slowly from a jar?

This is a honeybee's honey.

Isn't it yummy? Honeybees think so, too. During the summer, busy bees make honey from the nectar of flowers. They store the honey in their beehive. Bees eat the honey during the long, cold winter.

Fun fact: Between 50,000 and 60,000 bees live together in one colony.

Whose work is this, helping to soften sore hands?

7

This is a sheep's lanolin.

Lanolin is the oil on a sheep's hair. People use it to make lotion. Slippery lanolin waterproofs a sheep's wool coat. The sheep can spend long days in a rainy pasture without getting its skin wet.

Fun fact: To shear a sheep means to cut its wool—just like a haircut. A sheep is sheared once a year to get the wool and lanolin.

8

Whose work is this, covering a bed to make it warm?

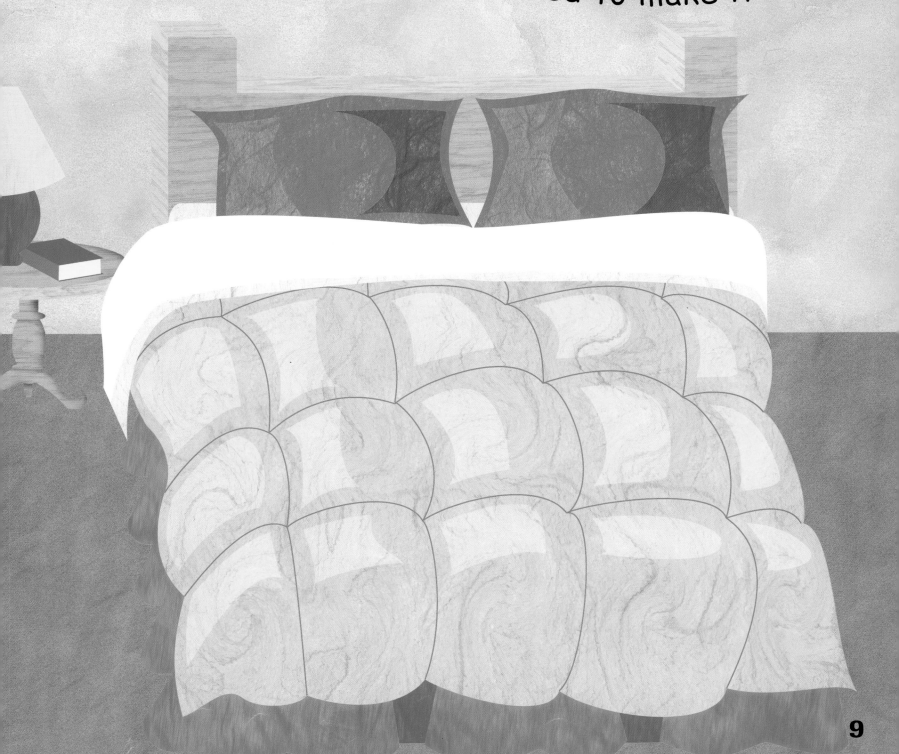

This is a Canada goose's down.

The down in a cozy blanket comes from the fluffy feathers of a goose. When the goose makes a nest, it lines the inside with feathers called down. The soft, warm down makes a cozy place for the goose's eggs to rest until they are ready to hatch.

Fun fact: A female goose will cover her eggs with her down if she needs to leave the nest for awhile.

Whose work is this,
catching swirls of light on a ring?

This is an oyster's pearl.

Isn't it pretty? A pearl starts out as an itchy grain of sand inside an oyster's shell. To protect itself from the rough sand, the oyster makes a hard, smooth layer called nacre around the grain of sand. The nacre-covered sand becomes a pearl.

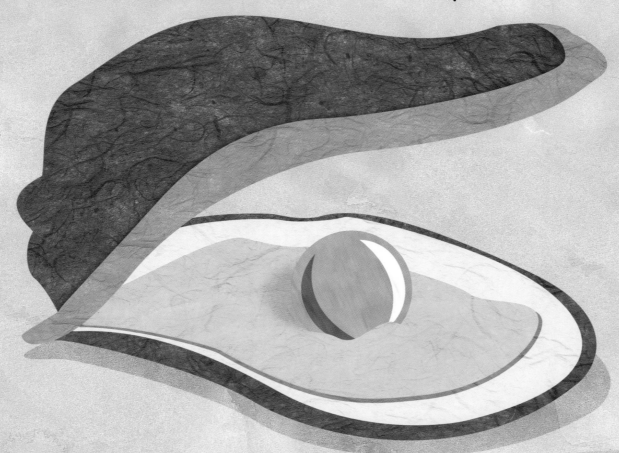

Fun fact: It can take as long as three years for an oyster to make one pearl.

Whose work is this,
being used for a shot?

This is a shot of death adder's venom.

This snake uses its deadly venom to kill its prey. The venom can also be used to save lives. People use the venom to make medicine for healing snake bites.

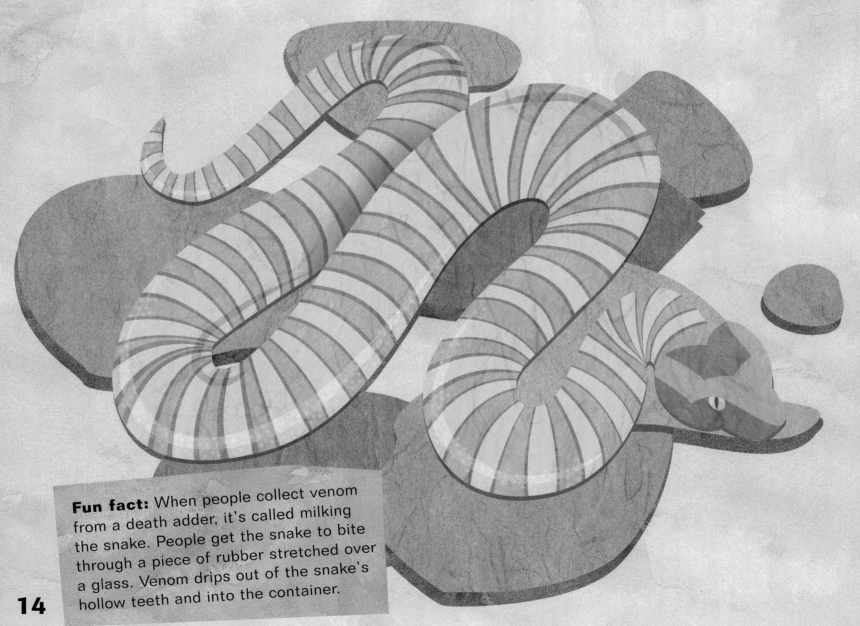

Fun fact: When people collect venom from a death adder, it's called milking the snake. People get the snake to bite through a piece of rubber stretched over a glass. Venom drips out of the snake's hollow teeth and into the container.

14

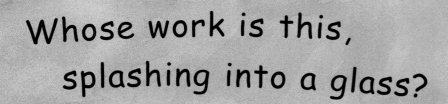

Whose work is this,
splashing into a glass?

This is a goat's milk.

Throughout the world, more people drink goat's milk than cow's milk. They taste a lot alike. People make butter, cheese, and ice cream from goat's milk. Mother goats feed the milk to their babies.

Fun fact: Goat's milk is easier to digest than cow's milk. Some people who can't drink cow's milk can drink goat's milk instead.

Whose work is this, sizzling in a skillet?

This is a chicken's egg.

Cluck, cluck. A female chicken, or hen, can lay one egg a day. A hen with white feathers lays white eggs. A hen with red feathers lays brown eggs. White and brown eggs taste the same, and people like to eat both kinds.

Fun fact: The average person in the United States eats about one egg a day. That means for every person in the country, there's a hen hard at work.

18

Whose work is this, hanging on the wall?

19

This is your picture!

Do you doodle or draw? Do you paint or write poems? Do you put things together or take things apart? Your work tells a lot about you. The work you do is different from anyone else's because you do it your way.

Fun fact: Everything people make begins with an idea—every toy, every game, every song, and every dance.

Just for Fun

Can you answer these riddles about who makes what?

* My oily hair keeps me dry.

  Who am I?   sheep

* I work all summer to make a sweet treat.

  Who am I?   honeybee

* I can make a jewel from a grain of sand.

  Who am I?   oyster

21

Fun Facts About the Work Animals Do

Mouthwatering Soup

Some restaurants serve a type of soup called bird's nest soup. It's made with a real bird's nest, though not the kind you'd see in your backyard. A bird called a swiftlet makes a nest with its hardened spit. The soup is made from this nest.

Amazing Web

Each type of spider spins its own kind of web. The Nephila's web is amazingly strong and flexible. The silk threads are stronger than steel threads of the same thickness. They can be stretched four times their length without breaking.

Pass the Eggs, Please

A sturgeon is a kind of fish. It is 20 years old before it starts laying eggs. People collect these eggs and sell them as a food called caviar. Sturgeon caviar is very expensive. Less expensive caviar comes from salmon, lake herring, cod, and carp.

Nothing Wasted

Cow droppings are called manure. It's valuable stuff. Farmers and gardeners mix dried manure with soil. Manure makes the soil better for growing plants. Cow manure is also used to make electricity. Manure is placed in a big, closed container. As it rots, the manure in the container makes methane gas. The gas is used to make electricity.

Useful Wool

Most wool comes from the hair of sheep, but some comes from goats, camels, and other animals. In spring, people cut or comb the hair from the animals. They make the hair into yarn for clothing, blankets, and rugs. Wool is also used to make baseballs and tennis balls.

Words to Know

down—the soft feathers lining the breast of geese; they use down to line their nests and cover their eggs

lanolin—oil made by a sheep's skin that coats the hair and makes the hair waterproof; people use lanolin to make lotion

nacre (NAY-ker)—the smooth, white substance that lines the insides of oyster shells; pearls are made out of nacre

nectar—a sweet liquid found in flowers and eaten by bees; their bodies turn nectar into honey

product—something that is made

venom—a poisonous liquid that shoots out of a snake's teeth when it bites

wool—a sheep's thick, curly hair that is used to make cloth; lanolin is also taken from wool

To Learn More

At the Library

Kalman, Bobbie. *The Life Cycle of a Honeybee.* New York: Crabtree, 2004.

Renne. *Animals and Their Eggs.* Milwaukee: Gareth Stevens Publishing, 2000.

Stone, Lynn M. *Snakes with Venom.* Vero Beach, Fla.: Rourke Book Co., 2001.

On the Web

FactHound offers a safe, fun way to find Web sites related to this book. All of the sites on FactHound have been researched by our staff. *www.facthound.com*

1. Visit the FactHound home page.
2. Enter a search word related to this book, or type in this special code: 1404806121.
3. Click the FETCH IT button.

Your trusty FactHound will fetch the best Web sites for you!

Index

Canada geese, 10
chicken, 18
cows, 16, 22
death adder, 14
down, 9–10
egg, 10, 17–18, 22
goat, 16, 22

honey, 4–6
honeybee, 6, 21
lanolin, 7–8
manure, 22
milk, 15–16
nephila spider, 22
oyster, 12, 21

pearl, 11–12
sheep, 8, 21, 22
sturgeon, 22
swiftlet, 22
venom, 13–14
wool, 8, 22
yarn, 22

Look for all the books in this series:

Whose Ears Are These?
A Look at Animal Ears—Short, Flat,
and Floppy

Whose Eyes Are These?
A Look at Animal Eyes—Big, Round,
and Narrow

Whose Feet Are These?
A Look at Hooves, Paws, and Claws

Whose Food Is This?
A Look at What Animals Eat—
Leaves, Bugs, and Nuts

Whose House Is This?
A Look at Animal Homes—Webs,
Nests, and Shells

Whose Legs Are These?
A Look at Animal Legs—Kicking,
Running, and Hopping

Whose Mouth Is This?
A Look at Bills, Suckers, and Tubes

Whose Nose Is This?
A Look at Beaks, Snouts, and Trunks

Whose Shadow Is This?
A Look at Animal Shapes—Round,
Long, and Pointy

Whose Skin Is This?
A Look at Animal Skin—Scaly, Furry,
and Prickly

Whose Sound Is This?
A Look at Animal Noises—Chirps,
Clicks, and Hoots

Whose Spots Are These?
A Look at Animal Markings—Round,
Bright, and Big

Whose Tail Is This?
A Look at Tails—Swishing, Wiggling,
and Rattling

Whose Work Is This?
A Look at the Things Animals
Make—Pearls, Milk, and Honey